I in the Stream

Poems: Volume IV

Glenn Martin (1950 -) grew up in Sydney, Australia. He lived in the hills on the far north coast of New South Wales for twenty years before coming back to Sydney. He has worked at many occupations: high school teacher, manager of community-sector organisations, psychiatric nurse, community development worker and social researcher, as well as being a writer on management, employment law, training, and business ethics. He has been an editor of professional and academic publications, and is currently an instructional designer for online tertiary education courses.

His previous books are:

Places in the Bush: A history of the Kyogle Shire

The Kyogle Public School Centenary Book: From New Park to 1995

Human Values and Ethics in the Workplace

Flames in the Open

Love and Armour

The Little Book of Ethics

The Ten Thousand Things: A story of the lived experience of the I Ching

Sustenance

The Big Story Falls Apart

To the Bush and Back to Business

They Went to Australia

A Modest Quest

I in the Stream

Poems: Volume IV

Glenn Martin

Published by G.P. Martin
5 Gumnut Place
Cherrybrook NSW 2126
www.glennmartin.com.au

National Library of Australia
Cataloguing-in-Publication Entry

Martin, Glenn.
        I in the stream
        ISBN 978-0-6480811-3-5 (pbk).
        1. Martin, Glenn. I. Title.

Book layout and design by Glenn Martin
Typeset in Palatino Linotype 11 pt

"I in the stream"? There's no "I" in stream.
It would have to be a river.

Well it is, eventually.

Contents

Preamble: About this volume

Note 1: The preamble comes before the amble.

Note 2: In my mind, this is volume IV of my poetry. In one sense (the literal one), this is a blatant untruth: this is not Glenn Martin's fourth volume of poetry. It comes after *Flames in the Open* and *Love and Armour*, so it must be the third. But there is logic in my assertion, although you may not consider it to be acceptable logic. If somebody bought this volume and died before the intended volume III was produced, there would be a flaw in the order of things.

Volumes I and II were conceived at the same time, at Horseshoe Creek, Kyogle, in 1989. I compiled the two volumes from poems I had written over a period of about twenty years; the two volumes were loosely themed around their titles, but in parallel over time.

Volume III was also conceived at this time, but not executed. It was intended to be a judicious selection from my earlier poems, judicious because we are talking about my young days and….

After rather a long time, I still haven't produced volume III, so volume IV usurps its place, at least chronologically.

Yet I say, unapologetically: Nevertheless.

I acknowledge also that the 'IV' owes something to Led Zeppelin. They had the cheek to issue their fourth album without a name at all, maintaining that people would know who they were by then. And people did. That was the album containing "Stairway to heaven", the album that had the strong lore (or lure) of Tolkein's *Lord of the Rings* about it.

Our days have been rich. We have heard glorious music and it inhabits the caverns and byways of our minds. We have seen and experienced wondrous things. Amidst all of the horrors, the cruelties and harshness that attend our lives on this planet, the bliss climbs to the stars and shines out of deep sky. All of this we have imbibed and it dwells within us. It is the bliss we must coax again into the doorway.

Note 3: Why the title? Like much of what happens in poetry, the phrase just came to me, and I liked it. We all have a bank of elemental concepts that float around our minds (both physical – like earth, mountain, ocean, tree – and abstract, like large, and force, and gentle). And occasionally, phrases emerge out of the constant buzz and flow of these concepts.

The phrase seemed to articulate nicely what I was doing – looking back into the stream of my own life and picking out pieces that were floating by (leaves, twigs) to enjoy, and to wonder about once more.

Note 4: What is to be said about the content of *I in the Stream*? I say this: We are of the spirit. We are not machines. We may have become quite good at being machines, but without spirit we die, or at least, we render life into a state where it is difficult for us to muster meaning or joy.

The cat that purrs in the doorway while it is watching traffic is not executing a plan; the purring is the full and complete message. Or, the purring ceases precisely at the moment it even becomes a message.

My poems are just a cat watching the traffic. I am making sense of experience: "and on good days, we run together".

Note 5: Quirks

There are a couple of poems that may not be poems. They could be discursive dissertations about poetry. I don't care. I think I proved to myself in these experiences that the boundary between prose and poetry can become porous. It is the kind of territory where unicorns can pass across, and guards from either side of the border are powerless to prevent it.

"This is a moment.
You will need A4 paper, and any kind of pen.
I don't care if you drink or not.
I don't care if you laugh or cry.
I only beseech you to get to the other side."

Note 6: I am struck by the unevenness of this poetic endeavour. The dates give me away. And there is the other side of disclosure – context. As a critic of an instance of particularly bad philosophy, I said: "Text without context is a con."

I am sometimes frustrated by poetry books that offer only the poems, as if the context was always either self-evident or irrelevant, or as if the words were always shining pronouncements from an exalted plane. Yes, sometimes context fades and becomes irrelevant, and only the universal truth remains, but often, knowing the context helps you to see inside the meaning. Mine is a modest endeavor, and sometimes the parameters of my exercises need to be spelled out.

For example. The "Five words" poetry workshop occurred because I was reading Stephen Harrod Buhner's book, *Ensouling Language: On the art of nonfiction and the writer's life.* I was staying at my mother's house in Ballina. I had just taken her down to Sydney to a nursing home, so she would be nearer to me, and I had her house on the market. I had to start cleaning out the house, going through her possessions and packing up what was to be kept.

I was there for several days, alone, so Buhner's book on writing non-fiction from a spirit perspective lobbed into my mental space like a bomb: "I wasn't prepared".

I hadn't tried to make sense of my life like that before. I mean, the idea of my life as a writer, and a writer's experience of life; indeed, the obligations of such a life. So, I carried out the workshop exercise he proposed, over several hours one afternoon out the back of mum's house under a large sky. The sun went down and the moon came out.

Shortly before my mother died, I showed her the latest book I had written. She was never going to read it, but she said, "You always were good with words".

And this volume contains another poem about poetry ("Workshop on poetry"). It was an actual workshop, at the New South Wales Writers' Centre. There, the poet MTC Cronin (Margaret) had us address the question of what poetry is. I was interested. At the time, I was writing articles and commentary on prosaic subjects such as management, training, employment law and business ethics.

At the same time, I was occasionally assailed by the "crude flush of words" that poetry can be. The soft boundary to the land of poetry was persistently present. It infiltrated. It stood next to me in serious moments and said, inappropriately, "Poetry is the shape of sky".

Note 7: The dates on the poems

I know, I don't have to do it, and few poets do. But it's evidence and it's context, and it may illuminate something that I haven't thought of yet. Sure, it may not matter, but it's true: some of these poems happened in rapid succession, and there have been long gaps between other poems.

I have had gainful occupations; I am only intermittently a poet. But there have often been times when I have rubbed shoulders with luminous words and phrases, generally at times when I have been endeavouring to be sensible.

Note 8: Which is my favourite poem?

Your choices may be different to mine; I expect so. For me, "I live in the city" was epochal, and I am still living in that sensibility after twenty years of being back in the city (it was 2008 when I wrote it, more than ten years after I came back to Sydney). (I find it astounding how long a current can run underground before it surfaces, like the freesias that have bloomed along my driveway after 15 years.)

And "Kookaburra (2)". I decided years ago, indigenous fashion, that the kookaburra was my totem animal, and a kookaburra comes to sit on my fence regularly, sometimes with its partner. It looks me in the eye and I say: "Nevertheless. I am here".

Note 9: I realise that I am still being sparing with context. But you know I will make no apology for that. I will write an afterword. I will try, but not too hard. Enjoy.

> *The great enterprise can never be truly exhausted.*
> *Souls and spirits enter the great stream. Gather*
> *your energy to make the decisive move. The dragon*
> *is released from the river of ghosts.*

Cherrybrook (Sydney), August 2017

I see it
slowly –
it is a small book,
like a secret,
something that can be kept safe
from the brash light
of the world we deem necessary.

Writing your own story

To write your own story, start with the smallest and most immediate things.

I start this way:

> I am
> breathing in and breathing out.
> I am okay.
> And everything is okay.
> I say that.
> And if there is any doubt,
> I breathe in and out,
> I say: I am okay,
> and there are no boundaries here:
> so everything is okay.
> I am everything
> and everything is okay.

So the first thing that I do is to say, to say the obvious: I am, and to say what follows – it is okay – I am okay. And then there is – everything, and I say, I say it: everything is okay.

But the story – my story, and your story – is always longer, because we look out and see that we are embedded in the world, and it is immense and multi-layered. Someone has already given us a name and a place to learn to belong to, in contexts we haven't even fathomed yet.

Values, relationships, circumstances have been contrived for us, and expectations. We dwell amid this host.

So, the smallest and most immediate thing becomes like a waif in need of a parent, in need of nurturing. But, you are in a story, and if you don't write it, it will be cobbled together for you by default, by conventions and your acquiescence, by the long and weighty history of your ancestors.

That small and immediate thing, your consciousness, must contend with the world, and/or attain some sense of congenial belonging. Thus the story begins, it starts to take urgent and difficult shape. It becomes a question of what you accept and reject, what you move towards or avoid, and what you do in sudden moments when something great, for which you have no precedents or preparation, occurs. You don't even know the extent of it at the time. It is in retrospect that you see the distinctiveness of it, and its irrevocability.

Your story will have elements like this – a struggle with circumstances in which you are implicated. You chose. And yet, you will say, you did not know or realise what it was you were choosing.

At this point, perhaps, it does not seem like your story. It is a disaster that doesn't belong to you, that wasn't meant to happen, certainly not to you. At this point, perhaps, it is not so easy to breathe in and out. Your breath is constricted, crushed. And if someone else was writing your story now, that is how they might describe it: "His breath was constricted, his breath heaved effortfully beneath the weight of his choices and circumstances."

But the story is still yours. The next sentence is yours. The only rule I make is that the story has to acknowledge your experiences. It has to ring true. In great pain and despair, I have written the next sentence this way:

> I am
> breathing in and breathing out,
> and there is a sense in which
> I am okay, and everything is okay.

That is all I could venture, that there was a sense in which it was all okay. And I have looked for things that were okay, and especially, things that are constantly okay. I found a tree that was one hundred years old, that had seen a hundred seasons of wet and dry and cold and heat, and it stood tall and spreading, a shape that embraced sky and field. I have accepted the grace of its constancy.

I have made amends and started anew. I have stood taller. I have found that the bad stories may stay in your memory but they lose their power, because you know that you would not go there again. You would be straighter, fiercer and, withal, compassionate. And in small ways, it may seem, you begin to become the self that you might choose to be.

You are not the master of your story, because that is still largely in the hands of the world, but you are becoming a fair companion of the world.

My story becomes this:

> I am a fair companion of the world,
> I nudge the wheel
> and it spins out
> prayers for the meek
> and this is how
> everything is okay.

29 September 2015

Five words: The poetry workshop

This is a poetry workshop.
I wasn't warned.
I was only asked to think of five words –
Five words that were significant to my life.
I did.
It was interesting.
Four words that made sense (to me)
and one surprise.
Then I was told about the poetry workshop.
I had to go and look for A4 pages.
I knew that only that would do.

"Write five poems", the man said.
"Okay", I think. One on each word.
But "No", he says. "You must have
all five words
in each poem."

I think, overkill.
What would be the point?
I could use carbon paper, make carbon copies.
I could press really hard on the paper.

"No", he says. "Five poems, and…"
Yes, I know. The five words have to be
in each of the five poems.
How long do I have?
"Forever, but start now."

I can manage one poem, I think.
At least, I know how it starts.

I will tell you the challenge, the words: 1 Say, 2 Stand, 3 Aim, 4
See, 5 Gather.
So here is my first poem.

Poem 1

In short pants, I learned that I could **say**.
It seemed to be something exceptional,
so I was asked to say, often.
"Write something about nature.
Bushrangers.
Write a ballad. Make it rhyme.
Write modern verse – make it without rhyme,
but so we still know it's a poem."
I could say, with occasional delight,
but mostly like rock, with just
a rare vein of ore to requite.

I learned that I needed to **stand**.
He had explained that. He called it hatred
but that was just for dramatic effect.
He hated torture, greed, abuse of power, lies.
So I understood. He was standing –
standing for, standing against, and above all, standing up.
When you can stand, you can withstand.
I got it. You can see how all this
is developmental (in modern verse):
I say (what?) and I stand for (and against).

And still I am buried in battles,
only some of which matter.
I need **aim**.
I need to choose battles, and learn how to decline.
I need to choose targets, and own them as mine.

I need to dampen the clamouring voices.
Then: the essential choices avail themselves
only when you can **see**.
I thought I saw.
In hindsight I was driven.
Activity is always a given.

I'm not sorry.
Without the mistakes and the calamities
what would I have seen?
I would have glossed over the flight,
unhardened by storms and majesty,
soft in shallow parlours despite
the best of intentions.
Seeing came late, I am sure of that,
and even now the ship is uncertain,
in high waves but with sails that
fill bravely. My prow juts into old winds
and, it seems, in this season I will **gather**.
I had not thought so, not even pondered,
but the harvests have been ripening.
We breast the waves and lunge onto the shore.

End of Poem 1.

Poem 2

Say / Stand / Aim / See / Gather

Having spelled out the tale
you think it would be clear
but the afternoon is longer
and the moon like a cup is at my shoulder,
low in the sky and listening, like me,
to birdsong.

Say: I can talk, I can talk into your cup,
I can even say that
the most important thing to say
is that I am listening –
to birdsong, to the solitary skink in the garage,
to distant traffic.
Is it important for me to say
what it is important to say,
or should I just say
whatever it is and trust
in the listening of the moon at my shoulder?
Brighter moon, paling sky. Clearer.

Such an hour to **stand**, as night comes
and fears are released like unseen devils
that chatter or hiss or breathe menace.
There might be sharp teeth in that shadow
that mean lustful harm.
But I know, I have experienced
the silent ritual, without any audience –
I stand. Feet on earth, spine erect,
head tilted just so – I defy
any seething swarm of devils. To the end.
When I am sure of this,
I learn **aim**.

I thought I knew aim.
I thought that that was the easiest thing,
the first thing.
But you cannot aim
until your feet
have found solid ground
and you have looked around
and decided what it is

that is worthwhile.
Then, and only then, can you aim well.

And all the while the light is withdrawing
and it finally occurs to me,
the importance of **seeing,**
but I am going to have to trust my body now,
to trust that it has remembered
all I have been learning.
Even the pen spiders across the page
(the A4 page)
in shadow.
The skink, the flutter of birds, the first star,
the moon enjoying.
It is almost too dark,
but in a clear sky
the bats are **gathering,** gathering,

that strange community of wings
that portends.....?
The sentence is unfinished –
What do I draw on?
Biology? Mythology? The prejudice of the populace?
I am dark. The page is dissolving into blackness.
I say what is.
How bright the moon!

Poem 3

Poem 3 is about endurance;
there will be no surrender.

I can **say.** Not everybody can.
(Sometimes I can't either.)

But there are different kinds of saying:
clever saying,
soothsaying,
clear saying,
exalted.
Rhymes and metaphors,
an arresting simile.
What is this gift for?
And am I harnessed to necessity,
a pay packet, a posture,
an accommodation banal?
So again, I know that
the thing that is needful is to **stand**.
And in time, I learn that
I need to **aim**,
but at what?
This is it: at what is helpful.
I leave the truth crusaders behind.
Truth can be an ugly weapon.
No, rather, I am at home
with what is helpful.
And this is what I come to see as **seeing**.
Of course, what is helpful
is what allows us to see the truth.
And finally, it seems that
it is a matter of course
that there will be **gathering**,
that all those small kernels of faith
in goodness
come cropping
and what was earnest becomes laughter.
In the gathering I am embraced,
I the wanderer alone,
gathered in after all.

Poem 4

Poem 4 is about the plateau,
peace and nurturing.
Up here we **say** little.
There is no need.
We are **standing** apart
and finding sustenance.
We don't countenance fake necessities.
Each day is wonder
of growth and harvest
and satisfy,
perhaps unruly, but the threads
have now loosened,
and there is no **aim** anymore.
Where else would I aim but here?
I **see**. All there is to say
is what I see, I can say no more.
And the **gathering** is what came first.
Everything proceeds out of the gathering.

I say the gathering.
I stand for it.
I aim at the centre.
This is what I see.
Fresh flowers.

Poem 5

For the morrow.
It is a certain type of truth:
themes for the endeavour of a life.
It came in this order:
"Say."
"Stand."

"Aim."
"See."
"Gather."

Inconvenient but natural, and therefore necessary.

And with just these words,
I burn down the building that is exhausted,
I thrust my hand into the sky,
I honour the dawn,
I ask if it is all done
when the land is so empty.
But five words came together
and it is not done yet –
my aim remains true,
I have taken a stand.
We shall see.
I say.
The clouds gather.

9 February 2017
Ballina

Funeral music

Death comes in many ways,
prematurely, or at the end of epic journeys.
Life may be eked out or taken unexpectedly.
Either way the music plays
and there is loss behind.
We stand tall, trying to be the brave one,
but we lean also,
knowing there is this between us all –
vulnerability and mortality.

The earth beckons and wins.
We watch when those among us weaken and fade.
We may beat the glass in rage,
on the other side of their pain.
In helplessness we fight against the patience
we know we must learn.
We do not want to be wise – happiness would do.

And death becomes immense, it consumes us.
What good would patience do?
But then, the music. Why the music?

Perhaps because then we cease to resist.
We lean and are supported.
Indeed, through clear notes and beauty,
it is so much more than mere support.
We are not clients of social workers,
we are not experiencing some psychological disease.

No, no. In that space we see
light at the peaks of mountains,

we see such joy it is irrepressible,
we know the body as mere vehicle and temporal.
We reside, we are real,
in the open field of hopes.

The best that we wanted in our life
becomes the seed that grew and fulfilled itself
in love and bounty,
and we do that in the company of kindred spirits
who salute our joy.

* * * * *

"The mystery of love is greater than the mystery of death."
(Oscar Wilde)

* * * * *

(Written after the death of a friend I had known since I was
twenty. He died of cancer, which came, and came again.)

17 May 2007

Truth in the midst of storms

There are wild storms
and I see that I am travelling
in a strange land –
In a crass world I still carry my heart
as an offering,
I am looking
for deliverance
while the clash of thunder
grows louder, closer,
the rain on the roof
is a wall of sound

I have no weapons –
none that would withstand
the blast in any case –
I carry my heart in an open hand
and steel myself –
not to be weak,
not to be needy,
not to be pathetic
but knowing

that the essential truth
stands unprotected.

25 February 2007

Sky at Central Railway

Watching the blue deepen
behind the clock tower
the white face handing time to the night

22 May 2007, 5.26pm

It was weeks ago. We were sitting in a park, sunny day, perhaps afternoon. You pointed to sky above city buildings and park trees and said, "Blue – that blue".
And now it is later afternoon and I am waiting for you amid city traffic and the hurry of citizens. The sky is blue again. Can you hear the quietness in that blue, so near above the to-and-fro of cars and people?

[Image (imagine): The clock tower at Central Railway Station]

Children

These words were spoken at a child's naming ceremony. You may recognise in parts the words of others, such as Kahlil Gibran and Rabindranath Tagore. I thank them.

When children come to us, we know them as blessings of the universe.
Every child comes with the message
that the Great Mother is not yet discouraged of human kind.
Children come to us quickly and complete, and often we feel unready,
yet their presence is a gift,
even through difficult or prosaic times.

And we know that our children are the spirit of life's longing for itself,
they are not our own.
They come through us but not from us.
We honour them by loving them
and allowing them to keep their own thoughts.
We house their bodies; we serve them by not imprisoning their souls.

We are close and they are familiar,
but their souls are bound for tomorrow,
their dreams are from a different land.
We may teach them
but knowing that their promise is to inherit the future, not our yesterdays.

The parents are the bow in the hands of the Archer,
who sees the mark upon the path of the infinite
and bends the bow so that the arrow will go swift and far.

The parents bend joyfully in the Archer's hand,
wanting gladness for the little one,
summoning music that the child may sing,
remembering to keep a light heart
so that the child might not grow older
and sadden in the ways of the world,
for our natural state is bliss.

September 2007

Responding to tears

For a lady

I am caught by the unexpected,
and I watch as you succumb,
tears falling across our conversation,
from somewhere else.
There are probably six choices
that a man in my place might make:
escape, assure, pretend, ignore
and two more.

No matter. I have said it before –
"Sometimes there is no Right Thing to do"
and I couldn't explain
what kind of love it is I have for you.
I must admit a certain fascination
with the mystery of your tears,
with the story of a man who peers
across five lifetimes to you
and arrests your heart.
The I Ching would say the Wang demon
has got you, ensnared you,
and you must disentangle,
unwind the threads. Stern words;
I only say what I have heard.

But I am not the judge,
not the voice of authority,
not the police,
not the critic,
not the superior:
and nor am I feckless.
I offer a soft touch but I will not indulge you.

I let you go and I know that you will free-fall
until you black out
and get up and do it again.

I feel like a face in a dark doorway –
I am ready for laughter, ready for dance,
ready to fly my kite in the wind;
the past has been too long.
I say: "Unmake the trance!"
Prematurely, I am sure,
I know you want to be there some more.
Separate, I insist on kites seizing the wind.
I can only imagine you
stretched out, giving up,
screaming, "Take me, oblivion,
I am flotsam after shipwreck."

And although you can never count on grace,
somehow you are safely delivered
into a peaceful land.
Honey and milk, another land.
Suppose you make a small start,
breathing out flotsam.
I imagine you breathing in heaven,
I am ready to see you dance:
unmake the trance.

September 2007

I live in the city

I live in the city,
but at night I hear
the sound of the mopoke,
and in the morning the laugh
of kookaburras.

I live in the city,
but it is an abode.
I sojourn here.
I wonder about the people
who see it like a prison,
their eyes focused on a tiny square
of barred light,
hoping for Noah's dove
to bring them a branch
of olive
from some paradise
buttressed by remoteness.

I live in the city.
I admit that at night I hear
the sound of traffic and trains also.
But there is silence in between,
and it is the same silence.
I ask,
is it the traffic that is silent,
or is it the mopoke?

I burn a candle.
The flame is steady.
The flame burns
oxygen and travail equally.

Travail withers in the still burn
of wick in night's embrace.
It is the same light.

27 January 2008

Kookaburra (1)

Every day the laughing bird has performed,
she and her mate in the gum tree branches,
taking it in turns and contemplating each other.

That is how it is,
two silhouettes in the early light
while I wrestle with implacable chores,
working my way through the stark
to find time for the dream
to get to start the dream
to make the joy, the art, the project;
it is the retreat from free rein
that I am accustomed to,
it is a battle of patience.

So I listen for another way,
a shorter cut
where I am emptied of petty burden,
where my painstaking, tortured limp
is visited by lightness
so I see it can all be different.

I look up at gnarled branches,
the glistening drapery of leaves,
the unapologetic rough string of bark
and remember that this was my first memory,
the grey, sprawling grace of gum trees
and the lesson –
just to drink in this cool embrace,
that this scenery is my natural home
before I have to be breadwinner, citizen,
expert, stalwart, conjurer, teacher, resource,

repository, leader, servant.
I have my natural state, my totem
whence comes my strength – it is
the laughing bird; this
in a foolish world.

June 2007

Love and proximity

After dark and between showers of rain
when the phone ceases and the television is quiet
there is the chance to sleep
and if not, to plough down demons.

It is the hour when soothsayers peddle their trite catechisms
and somehow I know the transaction would be tawdry.

At these hours I go alone,
not as if I were an island,
but cognisant of the hordes I have seen
shipwrecked at daybreak
with their whisky and cigarettes and embarrassing
sentimentality –
yes, you will see, it is sentimentality.

I sail true, eyes sharp for the shadows of rocks
and the safe beacon of lighthouses,
ears sharp for waves upon shoals
and so I keep my hull safe
to sail into harbours –
love is not always proximate.

18 January 2008

Articulating the crossing

How well the moon takes the sky.
I walk the shining road
to banish cloying dark.
I am imbued,
I would call it new light,
I step nimbly
and turn away from gloom,
the ready companion.
I take the moon's glow
to roam. This is new.
This is as if first time:
I spurn the sad verses
and aspire to a clean connection,
the moment that rides high.
Thus I cross the fearsome plain:
in hand with shining moon,
walking the shining road.

23 January 2008

Drinking coffee

It is as if I am drinking coffee,
sitting at a small table in an outdoor cafe
with an empty chair opposite,
a certain air of equanimity,
people passing,
sunlight and shade, light falling in colour
and the coffee is satisfactory.

I bubble with thoughts,
hear snatches of music,
the sighing of conversations, whispers, laughter
carried on breeze.
It's as if this picture, perfect in itself,
were an invitation.

I have laid down past plights,
forgiven unsavoury episodes,
partners gone, I concede I was unequal
to what might have been required.
I remember sadness, driven down my own paths,
knowing I was becoming alone,
having to venture without company,
and learning to disregard the taunts.

It may ever be now,
listening to the babble of thoughts
in my own company,
musing on my salvation from worse fates.

As time empties
there is less of the past to share with anyone.
I sit opposite a chair,

not five, when I was enchanted with the gaiety of girls,
not ten, when I was taken with the mystery
of one girl, silently imagining bonds with that loveliness,
not fifteen, when I was keen and aware
of prettiness and promises,
not twenty-five either, when I thought there was
a dream of gold to be spun true.

Aground, I have learned the consolations
of my station – I have not had to debate
brands of toothpaste
or where the table should be placed.

Is it strange that I drink coffee alone?
Indeed, I often prefer to do it at home,
away from the glances at a chair wanting.
It is worse when the question hanging is why
it is so when
I don't seem to be averse to company,
to talk or laughter or closeness.
I have to let that go,
leaving the question there,
not abandoning hope to strangers
who fleetingly care.
I savour what is – coffee, light, colour
and voices around,
it is all a merry dance of strangers
subject to dangers,
it is scenery where chance is a gift
and I am ever poised to shift.

10 August 2007

Perhaps pretending to falter

We always move on,
through evenings of wine
and mornings of new determination.
In some parallel universe,
artists are taking photos of us,
watching our dance into oblivion,
our striving for meaning,
our lunge, and our acquiescence,
and which will they believe?

I want to tell them they are wrong.
I want to tell them wondrous stories,
I want to tell them
that all they saw
was exterior circumstance
and that was their first mistake.
The truth is always well hidden.

My favourite photos are of pathways into shadow,
doorways into suggestion,
windows onto cloud, forest, mist,
and there I pretend to falter,
there I let them fall.
I am the real master,
the conjurer of elusive truth,
so unsatisfactory
in a product-centred, cut-down and tamed
version of reality.

The ultimate reality
is not wild, it is mild,
but you get there through the doorway of craziness,

you lose control and acquiesce:
you say, "It could be so";
it could be so.

You are not as authoritative
or definitive.
You are less grasping
and accept small mercies
that intimate greater blessings;
you pause in the midst of maelstroms
when the watchword is "Hurry";
it will seem like a dereliction of duty
and yet the dutiful have gone too far
down the pathway of duty,
egged on by those who have
no sense of duty at all.
That's why pausing brings you eye to eye
in an uncomfortable moment.
It is the sublime that I ache for,
not the menial.

Ah. I know that I have soared
and you will merely say
"He has left the ground".
But I have soared to show
the possibility of flight.

28 August 2007

Harbour city

I would know at the outset the essence.
In the event
there was dinner and not dancing,
there was quiet and space
amid the babble of Friday evening.
There was the harbour a stone's cast away,
light, glistening,
bright-dark water.
Hum, laughter,
visitors to the city
taking night-time photos in giggles.

In the event there were interludes
with waiters, diners, taxi-drivers, security men,
brief converse with friends
on mobile phones

and vegetables –
olives, rocket salad, ricotta and pumpkin,
artichokes and pine nuts,
and during dessert,
across the water,
the Luna Park grin

across rippling dark water
that was only there now to carry the lights –
red, green, yellow, blue, gold –
on dark water,
while the lemon tart and the cheesecake
basked at the centre of large round white plates,
haloed in mists of castor sugar

and I was always going home
to write the story.

June 2008

A recitation for meditation

I breathe in, I breathe out.
Breathe in, breathe out.
I set the omens at the four corners of the hidden lands –
I set the omen of light before me,
I set the omen of darkness behind me,
I set the omen of thoughts and thinking to my left,
and the omen of feelings and emotion to my right.
I sit within the omens, where all light arises,
breathing in, and out.
I sit in the golden light,
and blue light surrounds me,
I am protected.
I am grace, I am energy, I am love.
I make a new day.
Wordless, I let go of the striving
to be eternal.
Here,
still,
I am older than the earth,
infinite,
and days will take their place.

17 April 2008

Feelings and constancy

There are two things in life: feelings and constancy.
Feeling is based on joy,
constancy is based on correctness.
So there are two things in life –
joy and correctness.
And the joyful way is inherently correct,
and the correct way inevitably, or eventually,
is joyful.

There are two things in life: empathy and responsibility.
When the leader and the people are sensitive to each other
then their proper course of action becomes clear.
When the ruler and the workers are sensitive to each other
they are successful in their aims
and there is harmony in what they do.

Everything works this way,
so in sensing and feeling
we find what is correct, and
there is reason for success.
When feeling is lost, then joy is gone,
there is no correctness and no constancy,
and that way leads to evil.

Therefore, cling to feeling
which is the intimation of heaven;
be constant and correct
like the earth on which we stand.
This way, heaven and earth commune
and we enjoy the true bounty.

26 January 2008

The sober eye

After the day
it is alright,
the sun going extravagantly
in orange and purple, flair and flourish.
In the withdrawing light,
silence and two soft voices
on the western verandah.

Elsewhere,
the goal seekers are measuring their gains and losses,
the optimists interpose a "yet"
to all shortcomings.

Later,
there is a gathering
where a young woman muses
about whether the old two
will get together –
she is observant and good-natured.
But not tonight, no.
The old people know that distance is the victor,
laughing at it, calm about
the hazards of circumstance;
and the young woman may in time
share the mystery.

Sober, we drink tea out of
a merry assortment of cups.
Only Jane Austen would weave a future
out of this.

After the day
the sun hands over
its stewardship of the sky.
In the morning
when conversations have foundered
on clocks and commitments
it will say,
"I could not be there,
but I left you with my grace.
I took as long as I could to depart;
that was the hour of moment."
I thank the sun
for generous contrivance and style:
it did not go unnoticed.

Sober,
I count experience
like temple creatures
panting on the ramparts –
inexplicable and then implacably present,
no more possible than four legs
together with scales and wings
and an impudent face and fangs.
I go on with the ordinary path,
faithful, attentive, proficient.
It is alright, it is needed.
But I salute
improbable temple creatures
without reason.

4 April 2008 (Brisbane, evening)

Mastering days

The feelings bob like water,
the seagull sits like calm,
philosophy casts its net,
its words flinging promise
(it is all one)

In the maelstrom
and through tedium,
breathe in, breathe out;
eat, drink, in moderation;
do right.
Let that be your meaning,
return to centre,
let love shine
like a surprise,

like a rainbow
that smiles like
a leprechaun
leading you to gold.

20 June 2009 (winter equinox)

The shape of sky

I have pondered the shape of sky
poured down cracks between buildings,
leaning on trees,
a blank canvas for the sun,
a host for clouds.
I have seen the sky angular
and as the softest margin over far hills.
I ponder the shape of sky,
patient with the limits we set for it.

31 July 2009

This circus

This circus of thoughts
that comes of reading –
what one man thinks of concepts (versus reality),
what one woman thinks of memory
(a fateful geology or
a fond but desperate grasp).
It is all accelerating, it is
a madman foaming at the mouth.
The writings of men and women
are a thousand beckoning mirrors,
in soft light and harsh light,
from above and below,
and you know, eventually,
you will have to drop the mirrors
and hazard the broken glass
and worse still,
the absence of illusions.

Look
and there is the sage
at your shoulder.
Bewilderment and fate
are now less compelling.
You stop, turn,
you read only to hear the voice
of the sage
who does not flatter you
and who does not doubt you.
You see there is a dance
between fate and the sage
and you mark the steps of the sage,
to be able to be nimble yourself.

So you learn dancing –
from concepts to memories that are released,
from the comfort of memory
to the beckoning of a new future,
you are not afraid to step forth.

In new moments you know
that you must bring only your faithful self
that knows only the present
and who is prepared to swim
with the current
if the goal is everything
and if everything is love.

4 February 2010

Notes from a conference on spirituality

Baulkham Hills, 11-14 February 2010

I am not the master of the universe.
but I come from bliss
and that way I serve all-that-is.

What really matters is
to hold the centre,
to remain in light,
to be truthful,
to appreciate all,
to stand tall.

What have we found to be important?
Turn up. Be who you are. Create space for growth.
Enable the gathering. Be yourself. Reconcile with time.
Create opportunities for shift. Be inclusive. Trust.
Bring the spirit to the centre. Follow your own star. Love.

There are two core questions in life:
    How ought we to live? (the ethical question; Peter Singer)
    How can we become all that we might be? (the
    developmental question; Piero Ferucci)

There are two dimensions of life:
    the visible
    the invisible.

The tree

The tree:
blind channel,
a conduit from earth to sky –
energy streaming up the trunk,
leaves in the sunlight,
branches in the wind, loose,
crown giving shadow.

Whereas:
you and I are nothing if not an idea,
of spirit entering flesh
each breath
a journey of faith,
to be eternal
each moment,
both visible and unimaginable.

But part of me,
Nonetheless,
Is the idea of the tree –
up the trunk and into sunlight,
I have learned
that sap rising is grace,
and to celebrate
the wind on my face.

25 February 2008

Monk

The sun rises over jigsaw of buildings,
this is a season benign but delicate,
breezes lilting across morning shadows,
with young women neatly attired and intent
on making the office in time.
Around the corner a throng of early risers chatters,
bound for leisure pursuits
in a jauntily painted bus.

Breathe in, breathe out, sip tea,
stretch for openness,
stretch for vast goals, or none whatever.
Recall the dreaming monks
in mountains who, day in, day out,
committed the silence to memory
and painted the cherry blossoms for eternity.
Breathe in the chatter, the eager expectation,
and out, again.

Quell the tempests and carry the smile.
Today the monk is travelling
to a crowded village.
He will be watching in the town square,
observing the crows cawing
on scrappy fences,
and the farmer straining
to haul the obstinate ox across the bridge.
He will repaint the canvas.

4 April 2008 (morning)

Flames in the open

There are many ways of starting –
starting with a plan,
but sometimes what is given is
just a cloud,
feeling that has no shape
and I even hesitate to let it
assume shape.
So I start with a moment standing,
silence shared in the heat of a bonfire,
the logs burning as I count the years
since there was such clear sight across open ground.
And a log falls and splinters sparks
and that is all.
I wonder what it is
that makes monuments,
whether stone buildings stand
for the memory
of something that was wonderful.

21 August 2009
Wisemans Ferry

Pragmatist

"Be pragmatic."

I have a new meaning for pragmatism –
staying in the centre,
alert to everything around,
experiencing stillness
where I can see distance
with utmost confidence.
This is what works.
Holding on to steadiness
amid voices and clatter,
myriad agendas,
contests of perceptions
built on old memories
of disenchantment.
So, so and so.
And now I am not
holding on,
I am adrift, afloat,
anchored in the sublime only.
At one with deep sadness,
all sadness,
and all joy.
I go
along the path,
lightly.

24 February 2010

Workshop on poetry

What/why?

I urge to write.
I am wonder why
this sometimes crude flush of words

I see that there are two modes: poetry and prose.
I puzzle over that.
Conclude:
Prose is like an organisation – it exists because it has a purpose.
Poetry is like a family – it may accommodate purposes, but
beyond purposes, it exists also for no reason other than to be
what it is.

So I write organisations and families of meaning.
The meaning?
Image:
writing is about articulating the shape of the thoughts and
feelings in my head;
I strive to understand them by saying it,
by writing it down.

* * * * *

Describe this.

In any case:
The poem
is not the necessity.
The poem is
the other eye,
the other voice,

the other heart
that asks,
that looks,
that sighs.
It is ourselves
looking back at us.
It is not why,
it is, regardless.

* * * * *

And if I had to explain that?

We are the creatures of necessity.
Necessary workers, citizens, business folk, husbands, wives,
fathers, mothers, neighbours.
We come with ancestry and baggage, height, weight and
attitudes.
We learn – arithmetic, sentences, humour, humility, fear,
animosity, and sometimes grace.
At all times, whether we choose to feel it or not, we are in the
present.
And some of us are constrained to try to say how that is,
just as others sing or dance (or do arithmetic).

* * * * *

And my image for that?

Poetry is the shape of sky.
An image of the shape of sky on an afternoon.
Later, someone may pass by and nod,
acknowledging that someone, one afternoon,
saw a particular shape of sky and thought
that it was worthy of at least a moment's attention.

There is feeling in this.
Sometimes it is a wild eye
that is looking at the shapes of sky (on afternoons).
It is looking for what we are really looking at.

I come to joy.
If I tell you the shape of sky,
I look at buildings, and trees, and faces,
and see beyond them.
The sky.
Words scramble, stagger, slide into position at my feet.
Are they bewildered, amused, relieved, resolved?

I am making sense of foreground and sky.
Yes, I am resolving.
Among whatever fell along the path –
despair, angst, vanity, grief, wild hope, longing –
I am standing.

Then it is done, and the necessities are enlivened.

* * * * *

And if there was not poetry?

<u>There would be prose:</u>
I rake words into piles,
I separate and sort
to make tidy thoughts.
I am not content until

* * * * *

And what would the opposite of your poetic endeavour look like?

<u>Shake it off</u>
Let's start with an epiphany
and drench it with sentiment.
Let's market it with keywords.
The feeling will be effusive
(although the ethic will be conventional).
With bad luck it will relentlessly rhyme
and have rhythm like pop music radio.
I would deliver it to letter-boxes,
street by street
where lawns are mowed
and only a few stragglers
do not have digital TV.
And of course there will be audiences
who have cheered all through the rounds
of Australia's (or the World's) Biggest Poem.
Why are the lunatics
always starving in garrets
and biting the hand that feeds them?

* * * * *

(Poetry workshop with MTC (Margaret) Cronin at NSW Writers Centre)
Thursday 14 May 2009

The empty cup

Life is like this:
a sojourn in a café (a brief hour)
among people,
where some are working on their business,
some are posturing,
and some are on show
in order to attract attention, admiration, support.
Others are communing,
heads leaning towards each other,
lips hovering over coffee cups.
Someone waits on the tables,
observing the mood
and cleaning the empty plates away.
Outside the traffic ebbs and flows,
occasionally intruding with engine noise and sudden brakes.
And I wonder
what my labour is,
for I have not been asked to speak,
I have not been asked to write,
I have not been asked to lead
or offer a service,
and I struggle only to ponder.
I can only say what is insignificant
and wonder
if it is the best I can do.
It seems to depend on listeners,
but I am thankful for the coffee –
it would be churlish
to focus on the empty cup.

22 June 2010

Music as the journey

In the great sweep of things
John Lennon welcomes Christmas
and the miller tells his tale.

He is leaving New York
and losing his religion,
and I say I am not leaving,
for life is yet sweet –
and yet I am leaving, I am going around the sun.

But within this, we know
it is a winding road that stands outside the door,
and the door is life and death,
it is utterly simple,
so our song is best sung lustily,
for it is often a dark land
where I walk armed with whimsy,
around the sun and across the universe,
discovering the strange beat
of songs in the mist
and I must keep moving,
although I cannot see.

Dreams fall away but I know, I always know
it won't be long,
because things slow right down
and then I am in a coral room
with the embers of the night fire
glowing ever so softly.

16 October 2011

The labyrinth

In the labyrinth I learned
the sound of feet,
I learned
to put one foot
in front of the other.
The next step
is all the path gives you.
And looking up,
the people you see
heading in the opposite direction
may in fact be further ahead or behind.
I learned
that you need
to walk every step of the labyrinth
in order to get to the centre.
I learned pace –
when sometimes at every breath
you have to turn direction again
and sometimes
you walk for ages –
long, striding steps
until rhythm is natural,
but knowing always
that the path will turn
and turn again
until we arrive at the still centre
where new life bubbles up out of
nothingness – *prima materia*
to which I bring flesh,
and words to mark the journey.

28 November 2008

The handbook of Lu, the Wanderer

We are wanderers
despite the effort to be anchored in plans.
We are chosen to be in moments
we are unprepared for
just so we can learn to appreciate
that too, and that.

The wanderer learns not to presume,
not to depend on solidity
however solid it may seem.

We wander best
with simple rules:
To enjoy.
To act with correctness.
To be bold but polite.
To know stillness in movement.
It is grand.

3 October 2009

Kookaburra (2)

Kookaburra come look me this day.
No laughing, just look me.
One eye sideways.
My clothes line, his perch.
I say (no talking, just mind)
I been Australia long time,
mother and father, long way back.
Kookaburra, he still look me,
he no go.
I say, I grow roots down;
this home now,
nowhere else.

Next day I hear laughter in
old mother gum tree.
Two kookaburras.
That welcome call.
I stay now.

28 November 2015

Reflections on a story of despair

I watch the story.
It is someone else's.
The lady says, "It is love
that chains me to a horizon of despair",
and I watch her decline
like chords of piano music:
plaintive and becoming ponderous.

Others berate her:
"People decide their own fate;
you don't need me to protect you."
The servants may want her to succeed,
to secure the safety of their own lives;
just as easily they would want her to fail,
if it served the same purpose.

I see again how people create their lives,
although they are not able to control
the snow falling.

At the heart of it,
it would appear,
there is love;
either that, or the quest for it.

The ceremonies prove it –
there are ceremonies for love.
And snow, again,
and secrets, secrets we do not have the courage
to ask about; they remain undisclosed.

Remorse hangs, kept at bay, mystifyingly,

by persistent joy.

And the war comes,
And the war becomes a means
to assuage her despair.
In war, the borders close.
It is in this way that time passes,
simply passes,
although it would likewise seem
that some things are still eternal.

The foreground is all burning buildings,
gunfire and explosions,
rubble in failing light.
Screams.
"There are too many graves
for a single person to avoid."

But on a corner there is a blind man
playing the violin,
and there is the peace
each of us longs for.

16 July 2010
(while watching the movie, "Eva")

Science and the moon

The wind before dawn
sweeps around the full moon's face.
I can tell she is holding out to be aloof
but the leaves tell me differently,
they are pulling her into their scurry,
disdaining her claim to be implacable,
though I know she will become pallid
as the dawn bleaches the sky.

But soon, soon again it is silent.
(The leaves are off dancing in distant trees.)
The fleeting blush of moon is a thing of doubt,
and I am beseeched once more to believe
in the science of molecules and matter.

24 July 2016

Words

Words don't come easily [Tracy Chapman]
but experience calls for words,
and in inspiration, experience even calls forth words.
I look for words that fit –
the right words [Tracy Chapman],
words that say the illuminating thing
so that I can say,
and we can say –
Yes, that was it.
I am making sense for experience,
and on good days, we run together.

6 August 2016

Afternoon long and long

Afternoon long and long
Face and song come along
And say what is meet and right
All I can say is what I can say truthfully
And it may be a small audience or none at all
The notes are hauled up from the deep
And go out there, out there
I don't know how to judge
And of course that is never the point
I would rather flow
Go, flow, driven within.

Hey, take it on and onwards
We never can go back.
Afterwards, when the judgement occurs, it will be irrelevant,
Just remember that.
So still the songs come, and they reach
Upwards and we know that
Even if only for a moment, it was golden,
It was pleasing
And we meant well, there was innocence in it.

I hear of deaths, and they were inevitable
and I did not enjoy hearing of them.
They hurt me; I was never ready.
After the fall, I still want it all.
There were notes without words, indeed,
That is how it ended, just the music you could populate with
meanings of your own.
I soar again, above the muddling,
And it takes an acoustic guitar, the electronics take a back seat.
I am still not sure what I mean.
No, I know what I mean, I have that much,

I am just not quite sure even yet how to say it.

Enough, I murmur, sound-infused.
Ooh, humming, without the words coming at all.
Ooh. But there are always words, to snare the moments.
I could say, I have only come for the music, but the words tell us more.
So this is what I have –
In a long afternoon, music and musicians (I suppose they have to be called that),
Who went on a journey and disappeared, and who cannot be found now,
But I remember times when they presented themselves, wholly and magnificent.
Of course, now we only have fragments, but I remember whole moments.
What I remember is purity, pure hearts that urged love, without apology,
Without embarrassment, and without fear of cold judges,
And now it seems all the more wonderful for the many years that have passed.
And I know that it still happens, pure moments, just saying, just singing.
Perhaps it is in a small room with only a dozen friends, perhaps it is on a grand stage and
Nevertheless the story is simple, not investing in the grand charade but saying only the honest word.
There are undertones, we cannot avoid them, but
We are not distracted, we put the feelings up against the wall regardless.
We are not small, but if we are wise,
We know we are smaller than the earth.

November 2016

Family history

Beneath the silence, secrets,
things deemed too hard to say.
(Don't go out into the woods to play;
I can't tell you why, just obey.)

As children we could take this to be protection –
from danger, or sadness perhaps,
but we grew older and were never made wiser,
just at home with a false set of facts.

And the keepers of the secrets died,
carrying with them the comfort
that we were safe.
But I say we would have been better
in possession of the truth,
however grave.
There is something ground-worthy about truth,
you can stand on it,
as hard as it may be.
The first thing is having a place to stand
so I can learn how to stand up straight.

But again – soften, think –
this is how dark the woods were to them,
full of hungry souls and angry ghosts.
In dying they hoped to kill the secrets,
for us, to save us,
from danger, from sadness.

But I have dug up the bones
and cried all the tears that were necessary.
The monsters have departed.
It is okay. It is okay to go out and play. (September 2016)

Nuggets and haiku

Nuggets and haiku
say with syllabic rigour
what arrests me now.

(26 August 2017, 4:00 am)

The zen cat

The zen cat at dusk
sits silhouetted in the door
watching the traffic purr.

Haiku on the bus going home, 18 June 2009

This

This,
and this, and this,
and this.
And I,
in the midst,
seeing that.

4 March 2009

Autumn's bold sky

With autumn's bold sky
and the afternoon's stark sun
I drive home, caressed.

21 March 2013

I struggle with truth and with love
and they are fiery combatants;
I bow before their contest.

Uncertain I may be,
and undistinguished,
but I am real all the way through.

My greatest foe was self-pity,
so I gathered
iron for the soul.

Sometimes when I wrote I was empty
and sometimes I didn't write.

It makes a difference
to assemble words
to portray the feelings
and even more to summon them out of the void.
Words go forth as legions
to parry with the sullen domains
and bring back the harvest of gold.

No more mistakes? Ha!

At the end, if there is gauntness, be you love,
cherish what might be, even now.
Namaste. (Ah, you see, it is enough.)

On show, be resplendent.
On reflection, true in heart.
Spirit takes the winding path.

December 2013

It will be as if

In the end it will be
as if I have been all your loves,
and you have been all my loves.

That's it: the rain falls

So that's it,
the rain falls,
and time lasts forever.
It could be so sad.
And yet

This day

1. This is all you've got.
   (This is all there is.)
2. It is enough.
3. Doors open.
4. What now?

January 2017

Weather report

A weak sun has staggered out of the rough clouds
and leans against the battered buildings,
regathering its breath.

24 May 2017

Cockatoo cavorting

The white bird was falling
Like newspaper in brisk wind,
Just long enough to taunt the earth.

25 August 2017

Afterword

In my previous two volumes, I attempted to say something about what was going on when I wrote each of the poems. This was probably mostly for my own sense-making rather than any help it may have provided for readers.

With this volume I have been wrestling with the idea of the need to articulate context. This time, I can see the value of keeping the mystery. When we dream of something it is perfect, then when it comes into reality it is circumscribed and invariably somewhat short of perfect, or it is only a limited version of the perfect. This is the double-edged sword of context.

Sometimes words anchor a particular place or event and that is all we want the words to do. That is their purpose. And sometimes we want the opposite – the sweep of feeling that crosses (transcends) time, place and circumstance. The words soar, and the ground they lifted off from no longer matters.

And sometimes we are not sure which way the ground is falling, and then I have to remember: it is my book and I must keep my balance.

These poems were written between 2007 and 2017, mostly but not entirely in Sydney, mostly but not entirely at home. Beyond this, I am going to retreat from particularity. I will say, of these poems, "Everything is real". The people are real; I ventured inside the circle of their consciousness, or it may have been the other way around. It's often hard to say, and in any case, I never knew what I was going to say. And there was always something at stake.

Like the monk, I continue to repaint the canvas. And I try to remember: "The ox is slow, but the earth is patient".

In the end the words
will have to fit on the pages.
I accept the constraint.

Words are like a flock of birds. When a flock of birds
flies into a tree, the tree is still a tree, but it starts to
look rather more like a flock of birds.